TAKE BACK
CONTROL
OF
YOUR LIFE
now!

SO YOU CAN ENJOY MORE BALANCE,
HEALTHY RELATIONSHIPS AND HAPPINESS

ANNE MCKEOWN
2020 AUSTRALIA

Copyright © 2020 Anne McKeown

All rights reserved. No part of this publication may be reproduced, distributed or transmitted in any form or by any means, including photocopying, recording, or other electronic or mechanical methods, without the prior written permission of the publisher, except in the case of brief quotations embodied in critical reviews and certain other noncommercial uses permitted by copyright law. For permission requests, write to the publisher at the address below.

Anne McKeown, 2 Clavering Rd, Seaforth NSW 2092, Australia

https://annemckeown.com

Second Edition 2020

ISBN 978-0-6485268-1-0 (paperback)

Disclaimer
Every effort has been made to attribute all quotes correctly. Any misattributions are unintentional.

Contents

Chapter 1 Out of control 1

Chapter 2 Who is in control? 7

Chapter 3 Present and future 19

Chapter 4 I can see clearly now! 29

Chapter 5 Making sense of your world 41

Chapter 6 Inner power 51

Chapter 7 What do you believe? 61

Chapter 8 Goal setting and goal getting 69

Chapter 9 The struggle is essential for growth 77

Chapter 10 Life is all about relationships 87

Chapter 11 It is not what you say, it is the way that you say it! 97

Chapter 12 Let go and grow 107

Chapter 13 Track your progress 113

Chapter 14 A helping hand 121

About the Author 125

Testimonials

Anne is so approachable & positive; she has so much knowledge, and her goal is to see you happy. I cannot recommend her enough, she has taught me so many amazing skills.
—ZOE WIERINGA

Anne really is a brilliant coach, she knows how to encourage you in such a kind way and keep you on track with your life's goals. After only a few sessions with this gorgeous lady, I'm thrilled with the progress I have made.
—JANE KAYA

Anne is a knowledgeable, passionate and engaging coach who shares wisdom to enhance and empower women. A true leader of our time.
—DEBORAH FAIRFUL

Anne, your special gift, to show a woman how to manage and control her beliefs and simply be herself, is so valuable. Thank you.
—CAROL PARR

Anne, you were amazing, right on point and your message resonated with so many.
—ASHLEE TENBERGE

Anne, your heart and passion for helping women, are second to none.
—CATH DOOCEY

Anne is so easy to work with, she hears what you say, knows what you need and beautifully supports you through change. I highly recommend her to help you feel empowered and focused in your life.
—LISA COHEN

Anne is very inspirational and real!
—LYN SAVILLE

Since working with Anne, I'm more driven energetic and have greater clarity around my goals and immediate plan of action to build the future I want. I feel so blessed to have met Anne and have her as my coach.
—SHANTAL WALLACE

Anne is an amazing coach. Inspiring, compassionate and exceptionally knowledgeable.
—KRISTY SMITH

Thank you, Anne. You are the perfect example of feminine leadership.
—AIMEE BRICE

Anne is not only a fantastic coach but a very strong and compassionate woman. Empowering is the word I would use.
—KATHERINE LANGFORD

After only a couple of sessions with Anne, I felt a huge shift... she is just wonderful.
—MARIANNE FORBES

Chapter 1
Out of control

We know when our life is out of control. We see it in our self-sabotaging behaviour. We feel it as stress pumps through our body. We hear it in our negative language, and we see it reflected in how others treat us.

You may be drinking too much alcohol, overeating, spending money you do not have, or reacting with anger and aggression. You may also be blaming, shaming, or ignoring others, and even hiding under the covers, or nursing fear or guilt.

You may *feel* that your life is out of control because you lack time, money, or support. You might *think* that your life is out of control because you are trying to please others and failing. You possibly *believe* that your life is out of control because you lack purpose and direction. Your thoughts, feelings, beliefs and even the language you use all have a considerable impact on the state of your life. Once you begin to appreciate the power of these and use them to your benefit, your life will never be the same again.

If you are not in control of your own life, then who is? Who or what are you allowing to influence you, to determine your future, to direct your behaviour? If the answer is not "me", then it is time to take back control of your life.

I have had various times during my life, where I felt completely out of control. Through each of these phases:

- I was depressed.
- I suffered a crisis of confidence.
- I complained and then felt riddled with guilt because my external life was comfortable. Can you relate?
- I kept myself busy but was not motivated to do anything.
- I was resentful about putting everyone else first, even though I loved them.
- I lost sight of myself and yearned to find my identity and purpose in the world.
- Time was marching on, and I did not want to live the rest of my life feeling like this, but I had no idea how to take back control.

I thought I was the only woman who, after years of giving in all its guises, had little left to give. My self-esteem dropped. I felt misunderstood and felt that no one appreciated what I did. Not only that, I thought I was the only woman who became uncharacteristically prone to shouting and blaming everyone around me for how lost I felt.

When I first shared all of this with other ladies, I was shocked to learn that so many felt the same way!

I knew if I could find a way to rebuild my confidence and self-belief, I could work out what gave me a real sense of purpose and wellbeing. I needed to reclaim my identity, and without divorcing my family, was looking for a way to create a positive future. At the end of it, I knew I could help other women do the same.

And so, began my mission to create change and write a step-by-step guide so you, your sisters and your girlfriends can feel alive again and take back control of your life.

I look back on the years I wasted worrying about things that did not matter. The days I allowed negativity to dominate my life, the occasions I sought empty entertainment and the times I berated myself. Do you ever feel like this? If so, it is time to say, "Enough is enough. Life is too short. I am not willing to live like this anymore. It is time for a change!"

I cannot believe how balanced and happy my life is now. My marriage is better than ever, and I look forward to each new day.

A few years ago, I would not have believed it if anyone said I would run my own business. I also would not have believed that I would build a women's empowerment group, host online webinars, and live events, and write a book.

If I can do it, so can you.

My intention with this book (as with my coaching practice) is to firstly, let you know that you are not alone. I, along with the ladies in my group, know how you feel and are here to support you.

My second intention with this book is to give you tools and techniques that will show you how to live the life you were born to live and not a life you have learned to live.

You will start to become aware of your self-sabotaging behaviours, your fears, plus any limiting beliefs you have about yourself and those around you. You will grow in your understanding of your strengths and joys, your weaknesses, and negative triggers. You will also learn not to judge yourself anymore, but to increase your awareness and grow beyond these mental limitations.

Take a moment now and congratulate yourself for opening this book. For acknowledging that you need a change in your life. For wanting to grow. For being open and willing to learn.

But I must warn you that personal development is not easy. It is, however, essential. Others may not like it when you start to change; especially if you serve a purpose for them the way you are right now. It may upset their precariously balanced life if you have a positive shift. But do not let that stop you, those who genuinely care will seek to understand and be by your side every step of the way.

Also, a word of caution. If you flick through this book just once, I can guarantee that it will not have much impact on your life.

However, if you read this book, answer the questions, and do the exercises, you will feel a positive shift, and those around you will see the change. The people who currently say, "Why would you do that?" will soon be saying, "How did you do that?"

Are you ready to get started? I am excited to walk alongside you.

Anne McKeown

Chapter 2
Who is in control?

You cannot be in control of your life if you are not in control of yourself; and you cannot be in control of yourself if you do not know, like and trust yourself. So, during this chapter, we are going to search for YOU, the real you.

As a wife and mother, daughter, sister, aunt and dog owner, I had become so used to putting everyone else's needs first, that I lost sight of myself. Can you relate?

One of the things I have learned throughout my journey is that you cannot help others if your cup is empty. Some women try to. I used to, but with this self-sacrifice comes resentment. If there were a martyr reward, I would have won first prize.

Behaving like a victim is unpleasant for you and even worse for those around you. I want you to declare that you will start to look after yourself and take responsibility for your own life from this day forward. Can you do that?

The first step to taking back control of your life is to complete this promise.

PERSONAL PROMISE

I (name) ....

Am committed to my journey of personal development.

I realise that anything less than 100% involvement will not lead to my growth and success.

I hereby take full responsibility for my thoughts, words, and actions.

I am motivated to take back control of my life.

I am determined to do what it takes to feel alive again.

I am ready to create the future I desire.

Signed ....

Date: ....

ANNE McKEOWN
Empowering Women for Life

0449 571 974 anne@2mpower.co

We all wish to be understood and often get upset when other people do not understand us. However, it is difficult for people to know us if we do not know ourselves!

To find out who you are, I would like you to write down ten great things about yourself. You are not boasting, only you will see it at this stage, it is an exercise to remind your subconscious mind of what you can do.

Many women struggle with this exercise because, for years, they have believed themselves to be less than others. They have never been encouraged to focus on their attributes. They say to me, "I cannot think of ten great things about myself." Does this sound like you?

I became aware of just how difficult it is for women to invest and believe in themselves when I introduced the following exercise at the beginning of one of my workshops.

I handed around a little box with a lid on it and told the participants that there was something precious inside. I informed them that I only ever share the contents of that box with those who can appreciate it. They said they were 100% committed to respecting what was in the box. I instructed them to remove the lid one at a time, look inside, say nothing, replace the cover and pass it on. Those who got to look first let out a little laugh when they saw what was inside the box.

Those still waiting were intrigued and excited for their turn to look.

Inside that box, there was a mirror. The women viewed this exercise as a bit of a game. Still, it is a crucial part of any successful strategy. Your chance of taking back control of your life is not as good as it could be, especially if you do not look after yourself or see yourself as precious and capable.

For the next exercise, I asked the ladies to tell me one thing they loved about themselves. Silence descended on the room. There was a reluctance to announce self-praise. Everyone feared they would be judged. I told them, and I tell you now, "You will be judged anyway. So, you might as well hear criticism about something positive you said about yourself, rather than something negative someone else said about you!"

And I bet if you asked a family member or close friend to write down what they believe are your top ten positive attributes they would have no problem listing them.

Personality Profile

To help my clients understand their qualities and natural tendencies, I use a profiling tool called DiSC.

DiSC is an acronym for the four primary dimensions of behaviour: **D**ominance, **I**nfluence, **S**teadiness and **C**aution.

It enables you to understand your personality type and individual needs. It also helps explain why you react the way you do in certain circumstances and the reasons you get on better with some people more than others. It is an excellent resource for anyone having relationship difficulties at work or home.

This model is based on research conducted by William Moulton Marston and not meant to pigeonhole people, but to help us understand our personality and how to use our strengths to negotiate our way through life.

Marston was keen to examine the behaviour of people in their environment, or within a specific situation, and his findings are interesting. If you would like to learn more, he documented everything in the book *Emotions of Normal People.*

What are your top ten positive attributes?

1.

2.

3.

4.

5.

6.

7.

8.

9.

10.

Enjoying what you do is vital to taking back control of your life and achieving your dreams. If there is no pleasure in what you are doing, you will quit when the going gets tough. Do you agree?

We all tend to enjoy activities that we are good at doing. I would like you to take a moment to answer the following questions and reflect on the parts of your life that you enjoy the most, and which aspects give you the highest sense of accomplishment. Make sure the activities are evident in your daily routine.

What makes you laugh?

At what age did you live life to the fullest?

What do you most enjoy doing at home?

What do you most enjoy doing at work?

When people need help with 'something' they always come to you – what is this 'something'?

Values

In addition to understanding your personality type and what you enjoy, it is also essential to have an awareness of your treasured values.

Your values are the reason you do the things you do. They are your hot buttons. They are your non-negotiables when decision making. Most people are unaware of their values and the impact they have on their life.

Morris Massey author of *The People Puzzle*, discovered that our values are formed and developed during different periods of our life, and he classes them as follows:

- Age 0- 7 imprint period
- Age 8-13 modelling period
- Age 14-21 socialising period

Your values are your unconscious filters. They process a situation by deleting, distorting, and generalising based on your model of the world. Your values define what you believe to be right or wrong.

There is value in knowing your values, so do not ignore them!

Your values stem from many areas, including family, friends, school, religion, economics, geography, media, and personal experiences.

Your values can be different in different areas of your life. For example, it may be important to be loved at home but not at work.

Your values affect your choice of friends, what you buy and what you do in your spare time.

Your values represent what is important to you, not necessarily what you like. For example, if being dutiful is important, you will fulfil a duty even if it means doing something that you dislike.

What many people do not realise is that their values drive their behaviour, they are unconscious motivators and de-motivators.

Your values can push you towards pleasure or away from pain.

Examples of away values are guilt, sadness, loneliness, and anger.

Examples of values are love, freedom, health, and happiness.

It is important to realise that your values have a considerable impact on the outcomes, both positive and negative in your life. Eliciting your values will give insight into why things are the way they are in your life.

From the following list of words, I want you to select your top 10, those that are the most important to you as a way of living. You can add your own words to this list.

Authority	Excitement	Personal Development
Achievement	Fame	Pleasure
Advancement	Family	Privacy
Adventure	Friendship	Problem Solving
Affection	Growth	Recognition
Arts	Helping others	Relationships
Change	Honesty	Religion
Challenge	Independence	Reputation
Community	Inner peace	Responsibility
Competence	Integrity	Security
Competition	Job satisfaction	Self-respect
Co-operation	Knowledge	Serenity
Creativity	Leadership	Sophistication
Decisiveness	Location	Status
Democracy	Loyalty	Supervising
Ecology	Merit	Teamwork
Effectiveness	Money	Time freedom
Efficiency	Nature	Trust
Excellence	Order	Truth

Now that you have identified your top 10, I want you to eliminate 4, cross them off the list. From the remaining 6 remove 3, so you now have your top 3 values. Next, prioritise those 3.

Knowing your values and allowing others to know your values will bring awareness and understanding as to why you do things the way you do.

In addition to personal values, there are also societal values. Select the ones that resonate most with you from the following list.

Universalism: Broadminded, equality, unity with nature, inner harmony, a world of beauty, social justice, a world at peace, wisdom.

Benevolence: Spiritual life, mature love, helpful, forgiving, true friendship, meaning in life, honest, responsible, loyal.

Conformity: Self-discipline, polite, honouring elders, obedient.

Tradition: Humble, respect for tradition, devout, moderate, accepting my portion in life.

Security: Healthy, stable family, social order, clean, reciprocation of favours, sense of belonging, national security.

Power: Social recognition, wealth, authority, preserving my public image.

Achievement: Intelligent, capable, successful, influential, ambitious.

Hedonism: Enjoying life, self-indulgent, pleasure.

Stimulation: Daring, variation, excitement.

Self-direction: Freedom, curious, independent, creativity, choosing own goals, privacy, self-respect.

Chapter 3
Present and future

At some point in life, we have all made unconscious decisions to let ourselves off the hook or to give ourselves a break from responsibility and repetition, and even to be complacent or unintentionally lazy. Would you agree?

Problems arise when these decisions take us down a negative path. We become judgemental of ourselves, and our self-talk becomes destructive. We then need twice the effort, double the willpower, and ten times more positivity to push ourselves back on to the right track.

To improve your life and take back control, you first must recognise where you are at in your life. A great tool coaches use to help clients 'see' the state of their life is 'the wheel of life'.

I have included an image of 'the wheel of life' on the next page.

To understand your life, you need to rate different areas of your life on a scale of 1 to 10. Do this by placing a mark on each line. It is important, to be honest when you do this.

1 represents 'this part of my life is not working well at all'.

10 means 'this part of my life is great.'

The Wheel of Life

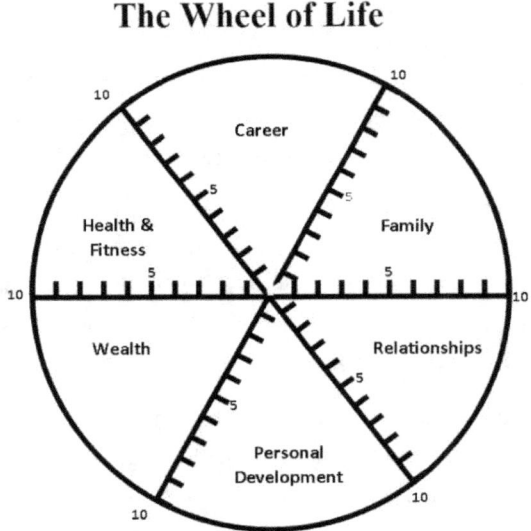

Then join the dots and see if your life is running smoothly like a balanced wheel. If not, this diagram will highlight the areas you need to work on first.

To help you, I have listed some ideas for each topic.

Health and Fitness: How you feel, how you look, level of mobility and movement, mood and energy level, nutrition, water, sport, sleep, stress.

Relationships: Friends, communication, colleagues, neighbours, communication.

Family: Partner, romance, children, communication.

Career: Level of satisfaction with your job, opportunities, social status.

Wealth: Income and expenditure, life conditions, choices.

Personal Development: Coaching, education, training, learning, volunteering.

Fun and Recreation: Entertainment, relaxation, travelling, hobbies, community.

Spiritual Life: Beliefs, meditation, prayer, religion, arts.

Environment: Physical surroundings at home and work.

Having drawn your wheel of life now complete the following:

Describe your life in one sentence

List the positives in your life right now

List the negatives in your life right now

How if at all, do you tend to sabotage yourself?

Now you have a clear idea of where you are at in your life. Let us look at where you want to be and what you want for your future.

What is missing?

I have had clients say, "Anne, I just want to be happy." Or "I want to be successful." But what exactly do these statements mean?

For some, the measure of success is by money and status, but for most, it is not. Over the years, people of all ages have told me that for them, success is a feeling on the inside, they find it hard to name. I call it *being you*.

I know from my own experience, as well as my work as a coach that happiness and success come when you tap into your true self. It happens when you like yourself, love yourself and understand yourself when you appreciate your gifts and work to your strengths.

Happiness and success flow with ease to those who are congruent. Yet so many of us spend our lives trying to please, impress or be like others, which is exhausting and not at all satisfying (believe me I have done it!).

You may find that you do not know what you want. You feel a tad dissatisfied but also appreciate that you have a comfortable first-world life and so you push those desires aside. Maybe a better question to ask is "what's missing in my life?" Jot down all the things that come to mind. Stop and do it right now.

The following things are missing in my life:

Why those things are missing in my life:

Whatever is missing in your life will be enhanced when you uncover your unique purpose. Abraham Maslow explains the hierarchy of needs. He believes once we have attained the basics for survival, that is, food, shelter, and safety, we crave love and a sense of belonging. It is because we are a community-based society.

It is a sad indictment on our society today that we are experiencing a loneliness epidemic. So many people feel isolated and invisible, and it is not just the elderly.

We all yearn to belong, but maybe when we built walls around our houses, we also built walls around our hearts. Perhaps unwittingly in the past, we have judged others and shut them out because they do not see life as we do.

When we humans lack confidence and belief in ourselves, we tend to retreat, and so sometimes loneliness can be self-inflicted.

When my children became independent, and I had more time on my hands, I found myself feeling a bit lost and lonely. Their lives were busy, and my husband travelled overseas regularly for work.

I organised my days by going to the gym and doing all the cooking and cleaning and grocery shopping. Still, I no longer felt needed, and I missed the buzz of the school community. I yearned to contribute to something more than just my immediate family. I wanted to be involved in something bigger than myself but did not know what and I did not know how to do it.

When I told a friend this, she suggested that I start my group and gather ladies who were in the same situation. The thought of organising this overwhelmed me. I had no idea where to start, and I was not sure I wanted the responsibility that goes with hosting a group. But at the same time, I knew that I was always telling my girls they had to be the change they wanted to see in life, and so I should do the same.

I procrastinated, as we all do, then one day I saw this quote on the internet - **If it is to be, it is up to me!** In any new project, it only takes one person to start the ball rolling, and I knew it was telling me it was my turn to act.

So, I took a deep breath and invited a few ladies to join me at the local community hall one morning. I was keen that this meeting would not be a moaning session but more an opportunity for us to support one another, share, learn and have a laugh.

That was in March 2016, and we now have over 500 members.

If you live in Sydney and would like to join us, we will welcome you with open arms. You can find all the details on this website:

https://www.meetup.com/Sydney-Women-Self-Empowerment-Meetup/

In the past, we have invited women who have overcome adversity to share their personal story. We have had experts teach us how to manage our money and invest for the future, how to look good at any age, how to keep fit and eat well, plus much more.

Some of my closest friends are ladies I met through this group. It was the best decision I ever made. I love it. I cannot imagine where I would be now if I had not taken that action.

Are you feeling a bit lost and lonely? If so, do not be afraid to admit it. I encourage you to reach out. You may even decide to create something in your local area. You will not regret it, I promise. Loneliness is worldwide, and no one is immune. So much so that the UK has appointed a Minister for Loneliness. Let us help and put a stop to loneliness by reaching out to others now.

Change is challenging

At the top of Maslow's pyramid, we seek self-realisation; being at one with ourselves and the world around us. We think of this as being in control, but it is more about letting go.

There are things in your life that you can direct and take charge of for example: which foods you eat, your exercise routine, the amount of money you save, how you treat others and how you let others treat you.

However, there are many things in life that we do not have control over. Yet, we allow these things to negatively impact our daily life, for example, the weather, other people's opinions, ageing, past events, traffic jams and much more.

Instead of stressing about the things you cannot change, I encourage you to focus on the things you can do something positive about in your life.

There are things in life that we know we need to change but do not necessarily want to change, and there are things in our life that we know we need to do, but we do not necessarily want to do.

For example, we need to pay taxes but do not want to, we need to work but may not want to, we may need to go to the gym but do not always want to.

Understanding the difference between your needs and wants is useful. Changing those needs into wants is essential. If you do not have desire pushing the change in your life, then change is unlikely to happen.

The first step to getting what you want in life is having desire. It is more than just wishing things were different. It means being willing to do what it takes to make the necessary changes.

Unfortunately, we humans resist change and thus make life more difficult for ourselves. We usually must be pushed or dragged out of our comfort zone. Many of us wait until something dangerous or life-threatening forces us to change.

Acknowledging that change does not come easy, that it is a process and takes time, is important. Understanding the stages of change and allowing yourself the time required to work through each phase will lead to growth and ultimately taking back control of your life.

Let us look at the natural progression of change.

1	Denial	I do not have a problem. I blame others.
2	Contemplation	Maybe I do have a problem.
3	Preparation	I do have a problem. I am in pain. Help!
4	Action	I have the support and a plan.
5	Review	I regularly track my progress and resources.

Are you ready for a change?

Which stage 1-5 are you currently in?

What do you need to do to move to the next stage?

Who is around that would be willing to support you?

Chapter 4
I can see clearly now!

I would like to share the following story with you. I do not remember where I first read it, but it had a profound effect on me.

Two women, both seriously ill, occupied the same hospital room. One woman could sit up in her bed for an hour each afternoon to help drain the fluid from her lungs. Her bed was next to the room's only window.

The other woman had to spend all her time lying on her back. The women enjoyed each other's company and talked for hours on end. Initially, they told each other about their illnesses. Still, eventually, their talks became more intimate as they spoke of their husbands, families, jobs, and personal life.

Every afternoon, when the woman in the bed by the window could sit up, she passed the time by describing to her roommate all the things she could see outside the window. The woman in the other bed looked forward to the one-hour periods. This was where her world would open up and be enlivened by all the colour and activity of the outside world.

"This window overlooks a park with a lovely lake. Ducks and swans played on the water while children sailed their model boats," said the woman by the window.

"Young lovers walk arm in arm amidst flowers of every colour and a fine view of the city skyline can be seen in the distance."

Her roommate closed her eyes and imagined the picturesque scene. Her smile grew with every new piece of detail. As the days, weeks and months went by this daily routine was enjoyed by both women.

One morning, the day nurse entered the room to bring water for both women only to discover that the woman by the window had died peacefully in her sleep.

As soon as it seemed appropriate, the other woman asked if she could move her bed next to the window. The nurse was happy to make the switch. The woman slowly and painfully propped herself up on one elbow to take her first look at the world outside that she had heard about so much. She could not believe her eyes. The window looked on to a grey brick wall.

What a wonderful gift the woman who died had given her roommate during all those dreary months. And what a wonderful lesson she has left for all of us. This woman understood the power of imagination. She had insight. She knew that the human mind does not know the difference between what is real and what is imaginary. It only believes what we tell it!

What are you telling yourself every day?

What are you telling others every day?

Are your stories positive and uplifting?

What do you envisage for the future?

Without imagination and vision, we have nothing to look forward to and remain uninspired and stuck!

Several years ago, I volunteered as a Group Leader on a project in Zimbabwe for an organization called SEE (Surgical Eye Expedition). I watched the lives of elderly Africans, who had cataracts in both eyes, be transformed from blindness to sight overnight.

An inexpensive, quick operation to remove the clouded lenses was performed. They were replaced with fresh, clear ones that opened a whole new world of vision for these people. Not being able to see held them back in life. They moved tentatively. They were afraid that obstacles might be in their way. They needed to be guided and supported.

What is clouding your vision?

What support do you need to help you see again?

If you do not have a vision of your future, then your journey through life will be blurred. You may end up aimlessly following the crowd and sticking to the same old routine. It is at this stage we become bored and dissatisfied, seeking thrills to fill the gaps. Those thrills can include anything from alcohol to compulsive shopping.

We attempt to fill an empty emotional hole by buying more things, but research shows that this has the opposite effect. With more things, we become more stressed, and we have more to look after, clean, store, and pay for. The more we have, the less we become.

As a young child, whenever I was sick, my mum would clean my room and say, "you will feel better after I have tidied everything away." And I always did; even to this day I still feel happier when my house is clean and clear of clutter. In your own home, do you feel content or claustrophobic?

The objects you have on display tell others a lot about you. The objects can lift you because it is something you like and treasure, colourful or modern. The objects can also pull your mood down because it was given to you by someone you no longer like, or it is dull, and not to your taste.

To help you find clarity, I would like to recommend you start decluttering and get rid of anything that no longer serves you. I know this can be an emotional experience for many people because it is about letting go, and that can be difficult.

Yale University researched this topic and discovered that the part of the brain that registers pain, is the same area that lights up when we get rid of things. For many people, clearing a physical path is genuinely painful.

For this to make more sense, it is helpful to understand that when our ancestors lived in caves, everything they had was essential for survival. So, they would be reluctant to give anything away. Without a weapon or a pot, their life would be at risk and less comfortable (no protection and no vessel in which to cook).

Our brains are still wired the same way. However, this version of fear is no longer relevant as we have an abundance of physical comforts. No matter how much we give away, we will have our most basic needs met.

I know it can be challenging to clear out things that you think you may need again someday, and I am not promoting wastefulness. But be aware that this could be a form of fear at work. If you have not used something for over a year, then you are unlikely to need it again.

It could even be a negative affirmation because you are saying, "I have enough now, but I will not have enough in the future." Scientific research has proven that what we believe, we achieve.

Thus, our thoughts become self-fulfilling prophecies. If you are keeping something for that eventuality then you could be affirming a lack of future abundance, so let it go.

My coaching clients often ask me, "Anne, how do I know what is clutter and what is not?" My answer is: if you do not love it and you do not use it – it is clutter, and it is wasting your time, energy, and space.

Allow the clearing out process to be fun and make sure you clear out with intention. As you push 'stuff' into bags and boxes to give away, crush all negative emotion with it.

Feel empowered as you take back control and get rid of the things that are blocking your path. Transform yourself as you transform your wardrobe, desk, and cupboards. Enjoy a new sense of clarity, confidence, and freedom.

It is important to mention here that it is not the actual stuff that's clogging your life, but the meaning you attach to it. You do not have to have a completely clear, tidy room, if you love everything you have and it all makes you feel good, that is fine.

And remember, what is trash for one is a treasure for another, so passing things on can cause delight.

Please do not keep old clothes that are too big or too small for you now. It could be a sign that your subconscious mind is judging who you are! Do not live for 'someday' live for today. Love yourself the way you are. Buy clothes that you feel great in now!

I had one client who worried that she would lose connection with the past if she gave things away. It does not have to be true. You can keep the memories without the things by taking photographs of items before passing them on. This way, they are no longer taking up space, and you can look at them whenever you want (which will probably be never, but you may not believe that yet).

Let me assure you that positive change will appear because you are creating space for new things to come into your life.

Visualisation

Now it is time to look to the future. During my own time of discovery and personal growth, I used visualisation as a tool to help me stay focused. If you cannot see the road ahead, you will feel afraid, and this fear will hinder your progress. As we read in the story at the beginning of this chapter, it is important and powerful to create a picture of the future, so the brain has something pleasant to focus on. This positive picture is what motivates us to move forward in life.

Let us create your positive picture now. Find yourself a comfortable spot with no interruptions. Allow yourself this time. You must be relaxed. You are going to daydream and allow your unconscious mind to come to the forefront and tell you what it wants. You will reveal your deepest desire and describe the things that make your heart sing.

Please give yourself permission to dream and promise me that you will not listen to those who criticise.

Get someone to read out the following to you – or record it on your smartphone and play it back to yourself. You will begin by closing your eyes. You are going to use your 'inner eye' to see your future.

Take a deep breath in and fill your lungs.

As you exhale, let your shoulders drop and let go.

Do this a few more times until you feel completely relaxed and comfortable.

Now I want you to imagine floating out of your body and flying above.

You look down and see your real body sitting below.

You feel free.

Free to create your future.

Ask your unconscious mind, what it wants for you.

You have a strong desire to find out.

You are capable and confident.

You fly out to your future, and within seconds a flash of light appears.

You look down.

You see your future self.

You are laughing.

Supporters surround you.

Everything that was missing before is now there.

You feel fulfilled.

You float down into your body in this picture.

You are happy in this picture.

You are doing what you have always wanted to do.

You are fit and strong. You never realised life could be this good. Take a Polaroid snapshot of this scene and put it in your pocket.

Slowly float up out of this future scene and head back to the present.

Look down and see yourself sitting below.

Float back into your body. Open your eyes slowly.

You thought you were dreaming, then you remember the photo in your pocket, this is your vision. It is the picture you embedded in your unconscious mind. It is the picture you need to put on your pinboard. You feel uplifted because you know your future is certain and exciting. Do not let anyone steal your dream.

The mention of a pinboard just reminded me to talk to you about creating a vision board. If you have never made one, let me encourage you to do so now.

A vision board can be an immensely powerful tool; here is why. The unconscious mind absorbs ideas through our five senses (in this case, our sight), and like an obedient child strives to find what we ask it to do.

A vision board has pictures, words, logos, quotes, anything that relates to your dream. Every time your eyes see these pictures, they will send a signal of excitement and desire to the brain. In turn, this lights positive feelings and embeds the message that these things are worth aiming for as they give pleasure and satisfaction, thus creating a positive cycle.

Looking at your board frequently keeps your dreams in front of mind.

I remember my first experience of using a vision board. I was sceptical of its value and initially thought it a waste of time, but within one year, I had achieved everything I set out on that board. Try it. You have got nothing to lose and so much to gain.

Pinterest is a great app for this on your smartphone, allowing you to have a vision board that you can carry in your pocket all the time.

When drawing on your vision, make passion your compass. If you do something you are passionate about, it will never feel like hard work, and you will enjoy each step of the journey.

And remember taking back control of your life is not so much about material gain, but more about creating balance, healthy relationships, and happiness.

When I do visualisations and goal setting with my clients, I tell them to: think it, ink it, and link it to all areas of their life.

If you are still feeling a bit stuck, and your vision is not clear, answering these additional questions may help.

What does my ideal day look like?

What am I passionate about?

What gives me a sense of purpose?

How does my work make a difference?

If money were not a barrier, what would I strive to do?

If I had a magic wand, what would I wish for?

Why do I want this?

At the end of my life, what do I want to be remembered by?

Chapter 5
Making sense of your world

We each make sense of the world using our five senses and our Reticular Activating System (RAS). The RAS is the place in the brain where our thoughts, feelings and external influences converge.

What many people do not realise is the strong influence our senses have on interpreting situations and how differently everyone sees the world and single events.

Our senses alert the thought process and create emotions and feelings that impact our behaviour and thus, the outcome in any situation.

It means that almost everything we do is based on our feelings. We watch a romantic movie because it makes us feel good. We buy a new dress because it makes us feel good. We hang out with friends because they make us feel good.

Equally, we may ignore doing things that do not make us feel good, and this can lead to procrastination and thoughts of failure and regret.

Learning how to overcome these feelings is a necessary skill if you want to take back control of your life. No longer allowing your feelings to rule your life as well as understanding how to shift your mood to a more positive state, so you can make better decisions and get better results, is essential.

We do this by using one of our five senses to create a stimulus and distract the unconscious mind. Let me show you an example.

Can you remember the taste of your favourite childhood meal? What feelings does this image bring forth? No doubt warm, positive, happy feelings.

Did you notice how quickly the mind took you back there with just one thought! Isn't that incredible?

Can you remember the smell of your grandfather's aftershave or tobacco? Does this thought bring a smile to your face? What does it feel like when you hear music from twenty years ago? Do you see how quickly you can change your thoughts and therefore, your outlook on life? Isn't it exciting to know that you can have complete control over your emotional state so rapidly?

Unfortunately, most of us, when we are upset about something, stay in that negative state for far too long. Or we try to ignore the negativity hoping it will just go away, which it does not.

Often, we want to fight it but do not know how, or we get angry and spiral further out of control, only to feel later, remorseful, and regretful. We try and tell ourselves to stop being so stupid, and we say it does not matter when it really does. These thoughts and behaviours can keep us stuck for years.

I appreciate that it can be difficult to shift your mindset on your own. So, let me encourage you to seek out a coach who is skilled in this area and can teach you to self-regulate your negative thoughts as you move forward on your personal growth journey.

Throughout your life, you may not know you have become conditioned and learned to respond in a certain way to different stimuli. For example, you automatically stop at a red traffic light, or you automatically know not to touch a hot stove.

The good news about this is that we can make these automatic reactions into a conscious process that helps us be more resourceful and positive. It works when a person is in an intense state. At the peak of that experience, a specific stimulus can be applied, and the two (the state and the stimulus) will be linked neurologically.

Have you ever noticed a tennis player clip her heel with the racquet before serving or a golfer pressing one thumb on top of the other before taking a swing? These are stimuli that they have set up in advance with their life coach.

The athlete will have been in a high state of confidence visualising success at the time of creating the physical stimuli. Every time they do this action, the body immediately responds by bringing those positive feelings to the fore and assisting the individual in achieving his or her personal best. Again, it is necessary to have an experienced coach to assist you with this.

Would you like me to share with you a way that you can deal with your negative emotions quickly on your own?

Firstly, I want you to think of your life as a movie showing on a TV screen. Now imagine that you have an invisible TV remote control in your pocket. This will be used as a positive trigger to tell your mind to pause, reflect and even rewind when you feel a negative reel of thoughts taking over.

Our thoughts whiz through our brains 24/7. Many of us are not even aware that these thought patterns are happening. One way to check yours out is to ask yourself "what genre of movie do I constantly play in my mind?"

Is your movie a comedy that makes you laugh, a romance that elicits feelings of love, a thriller that keeps you on your toes or a horror movie that keeps you awake at night? Are you enjoying this movie? Does it make you feel good?

If not, remember that you have a choice and all you must do is switch to another channel. You are in control. You hold the remote. Focus instead on something that brings a sense of calm and satisfaction, maybe a documentary about the wonders of our planet is what you should be watching?

When feeling overwhelmed or tired, you can choose to switch your TV (mind) off. Press the stop button on your remote control and do something different to quieten the chatter. Meditation and mindfulness practices are wonderful for this.

You can also use the remote-control idea if you are in the middle of an argument with someone and your feelings are screaming with frustration. Just quickly press the pause button on your imaginary remote control. Take a few deep breaths, say "excuse me" and walk away or calmly tell the other person you will continue the conversation later.

This way, you give yourself the space you need to think through the response you really want to give in a manner that will leave you feeling good.

If there are negative habits, thoughts, behaviours recorded on your film from the past, you can rewind and edit it or delete this content completely. These clips do not have to be part of your future.

The future chapters of your life are currently blank, and you are the author and director. You can fast forward and put positive scenes in your film. The important thing to remember is that you are not your feelings, you are not your thoughts, and you do have control over both.

Mindset

As mentioned previously, we have all been taught what is right and wrong by our parents, teachers, friends, and relatives. As we grow, these teachings become an integral part of our identity.

We, therefore, find it difficult when someone challenges these ideals. We often take offence and feel judged and misunderstood. Like the caveman, our initial reaction is to fight back and defend ourselves. Unfortunately, this protection mechanism limits our thinking and prevents us from growing, learning, and understanding.

Change can only happen if you are willing to grow, to learn new techniques, to try new ideas. This willingness is influenced by your mindset. In every individual, there is an infinite potential for expansion and growth. However, not everyone chooses to use it.

Carol Dweck, Professor of Psychology at Stanford University, spent decades researching people's beliefs around their abilities and discovered that it all evolved around their mindset. She named the two main categories of thinking as, fixed and growth.

A person with a fixed mindset believes that they (and others) are unable to change. They see things as black or white, right, or wrong, positive, or negative. They characterise people as caring or selfish, clever, or stupid.

Someone with a fixed mindset is likely to run an internal monologue, that judges themselves and others, by their standards. They tend to struggle in life. Maybe you know someone who has a fixed mindset, and you can see how it holds them back.

A person with a growth mindset is open to new ideas. They are more malleable in their views. They are more accepting of others. A person with this mindset will also have an internal dialogue going on but is more likely to learn from it.

People with a growth mindset are often happier and more successful in life. Can you think of someone in your family or friendship group who has a growth mindset?

You can tell if someone has a fixed or growth mindset by the language they use. The following examples provide some insight into a person's language.

FIXED	**GROWTH**
You are wrong!	Let us investigate
You will never understand	Tell me more
We do not do it that way	I am open to suggestions
It will not work	It might work
I cannot do that	I am willing to try
I do not agree	I do not totally agree

Have you heard the saying, '*Be careful what you wish for?*' This phrase is used to explain a phenomenon that has been witnessed throughout time. People who plant the seed of doubt or belief in their subconscious mind will end up achieving that outcome.

Modern science has since backed up this theory by showing us the subconscious mind, like an obedient child, finds and delivers whatever we ask it for. Another example is '*You are what you think*'.

What is your predominant way of thinking?

Has your mindset helped or hindered you in the past?

The exciting part of all this is that you have a choice. Even if up until now, your mindset has not served you well, you can decide to change it. You can make a promise to yourself that you will:

- aim to see the best in others and yourself;
- appreciate that everyone has a unique view of the world;
- accept that people are not their behaviour;
- admit that there are no unresourceful people, only unresourceful states;
- agree that everyone is doing the best they can with what they have; and
- acknowledge that there is no failure, only feedback.

You are in charge of your mind and therefore, your results. It is time to stop focusing on others and concentrate on your own self-development. Be a role model, teach by example and do not forget, the person with the greatest flexibility usually wins.

Chapter 6
Inner power

My teenage daughter was complaining about a list of things that went wrong for her last week and how other people 'made' her feel upset, or angry and frustrated. She was genuinely stunned when I told her that no one could 'make' her feel a certain way.

I explained that she chose her reaction to every single situation, whether that was an emotional response or physical action or negative self-talk. We went on to discuss the importance of her being in charge of her own life and the relevant consequences. I could see her posture change to one of confidence as she acknowledged the positive of having a choice around every aspect of her life.

Then just as quickly her shoulders dropped with the realisation that with choice comes responsibility!

Most of us are either unaware or unwilling to accept the responsibility that comes with taking control of our own life. It is easier to accuse others, or blame circumstances, or let our emotions take over and give in. This way, we may win a sympathy vote and can let go of responsibility. However, this is not the way to get on in life and take back control.

I wish someone had explained the power of the mind to me when I was a teenager. I never realised that every outcome I experienced was the direct result of a thought in my head.

I did not know that each thought created an emotion and that my behaviour reflected in that emotion. Try this example yourself. Imagine a colleague walks past and ignores you, what would you immediately think and do? Choose one of the following:

THOUGHT	**BEHAVIOUR**
She is upset with me, what have I done?	Be apologetic.
I knew she did not like me!	Ignore her next time.
Something has obviously upset her today.	Check if she is ok.
What a shame she did not see me.	Wave at her next time.

Do you see the difference in each of these scenarios? The mind is such a powerful tool, and we should aim to have powerful thoughts. Yet most of us waste a lot of time giving disempowering thoughts room in our mind and therefore in our life. I often use this quote with my kids when they are uptight about something: *'90% of the things you worry about never happen.'*

One of my daughters challenged me, saying this was just an old wife's tale. So together we decided to test it. For a whole month, every time there was something, she was worried about we watched and waited to see what happened.

The quote was proved true! Most of her worrying situations were either cancelled, forgotten about, or took a different turn. In 1948 Dale Carnegie wrote, '*today is the tomorrow you worried about yesterday*' and this quote is still relevant today.

Let me encourage you to make a conscious decision today and every day to stop worrying and start living in the present. Enjoy the gift of today. No matter how much we like to think we have control over the future, we cannot predict anything for certain. So, let it go and live in the now.

Just be

We are all aware of the buzzword 'mindfulness'. Isn't it crazy that we need to be reminded to stop and 'be' in our daily life? Isn't it crazy that we need to be reminded that we are human 'beings' not human 'doings'?

I would like to encourage you to put a ten-minute slot in your diary every day (maybe during your lunch break) where you stop and reflect. Make a conscious effort to listen to the sounds around you (preferably birds outside, not colleagues arguing in the office!). Look for beauty (art, sunshine, a smile). Eat slowly and taste your food consciously, think about the flavours being released as you eat. Touch the grass, feel aligned with Mother Nature, and stop to smell the roses!

During this meditative time, be real and honest with yourself. It is ok to admit that life is challenging. Accept and acknowledge your struggles. We all make mistakes and have regrets, and that is ok. Moving on is the key to taking back control. Forgiving ourselves and others brings many rewards, and inner peace is one of them.

Maybe unknowingly, you have grown to see the worst in every situation and do not know how to change your outlook. The following model was written by Martin Seligman, one of the creators of positive psychology, as a tool to help us deal with frustrating scenarios. Look at both examples below using his ABCDE method.

Adversity: you are stuck in rush hour traffic.

Belief: this always happens to me.

Consequence: victim mentality, feel frustrated.

Decide: honk horn, swear.

Emotion: angry and frustrated.

We can change the outcome of every situation by changing our initial thought. Let us look at the same situation again.

Adversity: you are stuck in rush hour traffic.

Belief: I hope someone has not been hurt in an accident.

Consequence: concern and empathy.

Decide: say a prayer, feel grateful.

Emotion: calm and positive.

I hope you are beginning to realise that what you think really does matter. Maybe it is now time to start thinking differently, especially if you suffer from any physical ailments.

Body/mind connection

Scientists have proven that the quality of our thoughts has an impact on our whole body. Both the mind and body communicate through our emotions. I said before, our emotions are a result of our feelings, and our feelings are a result of our thoughts.

In my twenties, I had an experience that proved this theory. I was single, living alone, overworked, and constantly stressed. I put my corporate job before everything else: long hours, no exercise, no downtime, no fun, just work, work, work. As a result, I became ill. I asked my mum to come and look after me for a few days (a four-hour train trip for her), and she did.

She was shocked to see how exhausted, pale, and thin I looked.

An interesting thing happened the next day. A guy I fancied phoned unexpectedly and invited me out for lunch – I was so excited. I leapt out of bed, put on my favourite dress, applied colourful make-up, styled my hair, and bounced out the door to meet him. Afterwards, my mum commented on, not only the difference in me but how quickly that change had taken place. Within a few minutes, (the length of a short telephone call), I had gone from sick and sad to lively and well.

The only thing that had changed was my outlook on life! The thought of a date with that guy was all it took for me to feel great. Our thoughts are so powerful. If you take nothing else away from this book, at least acknowledge the power of your thoughts and decide to take back control of them if they are controlling you.

Can you think of a time when your negative thoughts were interrupted and refocused on a more positive light? If not, do not be disheartened; this is quite difficult to do because, as mentioned earlier in Chapter 3, the mind does not like change. We feel more comfortable with what we know, even if it is negative.

There is a pattern known as *'the failure cycle'* no one gets caught up in this intentionally. Still, its lure is strong, and you may recognise its pattern. With every new idea, project, or prospect, you are filled with excitement. You look to the future with confidence and clarity. You talk about your plans and share your dreams with those who are willing to listen.

When the future arrives, you become scared and make excuses. You list reasons as to why something will not work, or why you can no longer make a commitment. You avoid the project and move away from it towards something new. Once again placed far in the future.

Why? Maybe your goals were unrealistic or unclear. Maybe you did not have a solid action plan to follow. Maybe you gave priority to anxiety, doubt, or procrastination. Maybe you are stubborn and have more will not-power, than willpower. All these mental barriers are products of your thoughts. Thoughts focused on past failures, lack of self-belief or old grudges, which hold you back.

When you block something mentally, physically, or emotionally, you prevent it from growing.

I have said it before, and I will repeat it - flexibility is essential for personal growth. Those who are open to change and willing to try new things will come out top in the game of life.

We all have the power within to turn things around and take back control of our life, and to do it today. If you do not believe this, then you may have unwittingly chosen to be a prisoner of your own mind. Clients often ask me to explain what I mean when I say, we have the power within, so I thought it useful to share.

The definition of the English word 'power' comes from the Anglo-Norman French word '*poeir*' which has quite a few meanings. The first I find uplifting: *the ability to do something or act in a particular way.*

I like this definition because it clearly shows that we can take control. We can choose to think, act, or react in a particular way, and we can choose to do something or not.

Often, we think of power as something outside our control, or worse, we see other people as having power over us. Does that sound like you? Take a few moments and answer the following questions.

Are you aware of your inner power?

Are you driven by your inner power?

Does it propel you forward because you love what you are doing with your life?

Consider if you are you heading in a direction because you 'want' to. Consider if you are you being pushed by force and stumbling along the path because you think you 'need' to do that?

We all know people (maybe even ourselves) who have withdrawn from a situation because of someone else's negative influence. If this is you, I challenge you to dig deep, find your power within and use it to springboard from your current position. Go from victim to victor.

And remember, you too can influence other people and any course of events. People who recognise their positive power of influence and use it for the benefit of others enjoy a huge sense of satisfaction in life.

There is also 'emotional power' which is vitally important. As mentioned before, our emotions come from our feelings, and our feelings come from our thoughts. So, if you are emotionally drained, it is likely due to disempowering thoughts. Think of your mind like an iPhone. It is active all the time. It is up to you to switch it off occasionally and recharge it regularly.

Most of us know the importance of balance in our lives and strive for that. When it comes to our mind, we let it wander like a naughty child, getting lost and becoming overwhelmed. We allow our mind to shout and scream and shut it down when attacked by the 'perceived' strength of someone else. Decide today to be the parent of your own emotions, say the loving things to yourself that you would say to your child, be kind and build emotional strength.

Whatever your spiritual beliefs, it is well documented that human beings find it empowering to know that there is more to them than just skeleton and skin. Whether you call it your soul or spirit or God or something that you cannot describe, believing in the 'spiritual power' within you offers great strength.

Chapter 7
What do you believe?

Early on in my relationships with a new client, I point to the floor and shout, "Look out. There's a spider at your foot!" Nine times out of ten, the scared individual will leap out of their chair and head for the door. Some are clearly traumatised, others puzzled. None ever say, "I don't believe you!"

Why? Because the brain believes what we tell it! There is never a spider, just a coach trying to demonstrate the power of one's beliefs, both physical and emotional.

I have listed below for you some important facts surrounding the human belief system and how it affects our lives.

- Beliefs can empower you or limit you.
- Beliefs are formed in all kinds of unconscious ways.
- Other people's preconceptions can place false limitations on you.
- Our beliefs affect our confidence to bring about change in our lives.
- We tend not to allow ourselves to want what we believe we cannot have.

- Our self-belief determines whether difficult tasks will be attempted.
- Whatever our belief might be, the subconscious will work to make that belief happen.
- If we can change the beliefs that are holding us back, we can change the way we act.
- Beliefs are generalisations, and they form our reality, which directs our behaviour.
- Our beliefs affect the extent to which we believe we can make things happen in our lives.
- Your own limiting beliefs show up in the language you use – I cannot, should, must, could, could not, etc.
- Truth does not have to be true or false to be effective. If we believe it to be true, it is true for us.
- Research shows it is our own estimation of our inner strength that determines our individual goals.
- The way to release our potential is to challenge some of the limiting beliefs we currently hold about ourselves and others.
- We behave and act not by following the truth as it might really be, but by following the truth as we perceive it to be.

Do you know most of your beliefs are based on things that happened in the past? Do you also know you are projecting that experience into your future? For example, when I was in high school, I believed myself to be hopeless at foreign languages. My French teacher confirmed this belief when she discouraged me from choosing this topic as one of my final year subjects.

Years later, my husband, who had studied in Spain, was offered a job in Zaragoza. The thought of moving overseas terrified me, and I cried as I told him, "I cannot move to Spain. I'm no good at learning foreign languages." He laughed and told me not to be so silly. For me, this fear was real; for him, it was implausible.

We often view other people's fears as ridiculous but take our own very seriously. So, full of fear and self-doubt, I moved to Europe and surprisingly, I was able to communicate effectively in Spanish after only a few short months. Besides, the locals said that I had a great accent. I would have missed out on wonderful experiences if I had given in to that limiting belief about myself.

Your life reflects your beliefs and the choices you have made as a result of those beliefs. For those who are unhappy, this is not comforting news. However, once you believe it to be true, it is an empowering fact.

We all know that we cannot change the past, but we can change our beliefs and create a more positive future. You can write your own script, tell a new story where you are the protagonist and decide the ending. You no longer must live the life others have prescribed for you. Some will find this freeing. Others may find it scary.

Why? Maybe, because you have become conditioned. Maybe because you want to please. Maybe that way of life is now a habit, and you have never thought of breaking it.

We all play many roles throughout life. Some are handed to us naturally, for example, our position in the family (parent, child, sibling, etc.). Other times we make a choice, like our career (nurse, lawyer, tradesman). Some of us even let other people tell us which roles we should play in life. This usually comes from a place of genuine concern where they believe that they know what is best for us.

Maybe without realising it, the role they want us to play serves them best. Some examples are a friend may not want you to have a partner because it means she will be left alone. Also, a parent who holds strong beliefs and expects you to do the same because he/she would be embarrassed if their friends found out. There is also a leader who wants you to be a cardboard copy of the perfect employee; otherwise, he/she looks like they are not doing a good job!

When we take on other people's desires for our life, we give them power in our life. Sometimes, we even let them write our script and allow them to criticise our performance.

Have you ever stopped to question the roles you are playing in life?

Are they serving you or someone else?

Do you believe the script you have been given?

Would you like to write your own script?

If so, what would it say?

What is your message to the world?

What is your message to yourself?

If you find the idea of changing your roles and beliefs to be scary, then you may be allowing fear to rule your life. Often people hold on to their beliefs, even if negative because there is something to be gained, for example, attention, pity, support, or excuses.

None of these will help you lead a fulfilled life. Be brutally honest with yourself as you answer these questions.

What do my roles and beliefs allow me to get away with?

What am I pretending not to know by having things this way?

What would I gain if this role and belief changed?

What would I lose if this role and belief changed?

The results of these questions can be startling. You might see a pattern emerging; maybe it is one of avoiding responsibility. Taking responsibility is tough, but we all must accept it at some point, and better sooner than later.

The word responsibility refers to our 'ability to respond' to situations. Maybe you have consciously or unconsciously avoided responsibility in the past and now realise that it is time to grow up and own your life.

For some people, this happens during their rebellious teenage years. For others when they hit the workforce, they become a parent themselves, or not until midlife and for some - never. If you have never had to question your ability to respond before, then it will be challenging to at the start. But you must start now if you wish to take back control of your life.

Choose today to create your future and the life you want. Like every author, the story begins in your head. Write one page each day the way you want that day to be and then follow your own instructions. By the end of the year, you will have an exciting memoir and be living the life of your dreams.

Do not overthink about it, do not try and fathom it – just believe it is possible!

That is what all world record holders do. And once they have broken a record, others believe it is possible and not only follow but push on to beat that record.

Now I want you to be honest with yourself and write down the limiting beliefs that are holding you back. Here are some examples I hear from clients:

- I cannot do that
- I'm no good at …
- I'm too old to …
- I'm a slow learner
- I'm too ordinary to have …
- I cannot drive in a foreign country,
- I could never do that
- I will never understand…
- That's beyond me
- I'm not able to …
- I'm scared …
- That's impossible.

And a final thought, if you do not believe in yourself, why should others?

Chapter 8
Goal setting and goal getting

In previous chapters, we have looked at who you are, your values, your beliefs, and what you really want. Now we are going to focus on how to get what you want, and planning plays an essential role for various reasons. It gets your idea out of your head and onto paper, which gives your mind more room to think. It is useful for sharing your idea with others, offers a step by step guide, a way to measure progress and a method for staying focused.

So how does one go about setting realistic goals? I want to encourage you to mentally aim high and stretch yourself beyond what you think you can achieve. This way, you will feel challenged and still see the growth even if you do not reach this stretch target.

You must focus on what you want, not on what you do not want. That might sound obvious, but you would be surprised to discover just how often we talk about the negatives in our lives. It is time to focus on what you are moving towards, not what you are avoiding. For example, rather than thinking, I do not want to be fat, you should concentrate on becoming fit.

A long time ago, I was introduced to the SMART model for goal setting. However, I never found the mechanical rote of 'specific, measured, achievable, realistic and timed' to be inspiring. These utilise the conscious mind, which likes logical processes. I am not a logical thinker.

One day, the creative part of my brain, thinking of getting on the right track and enjoying the journey of life, saw the word 'SMART' backwards. It read TRAMS™, and my mind presented me with a host of new ideas and scenarios around goal setting.

I am someone who has always been more motivated by my heart than my head. So, I made TRAMS™ into a template for 'Heart Goals' that utilise the subconscious mind which likes emotional processes. Once you incorporate both 'SMART' and 'TRAMS' models not only will goal setting be easy, but goal getting will be even easier.

When I share my TRAMS™ model with my clients, they love it, and I hope you do too.

Towards	Focus on moving forward to what you want, do not look back, except to see how far you have come!
Reasons	Why do you want this? Could also stand for **R**eward. How will you celebrate? Could also stand for **R**elationships. Who will help you?
Act As If	The subconscious mind does not know the difference between imagination and reality, so by **A**cting as if you already have what you are striving for, your dream will come true. Could also stand for **A**ttitude. Your outlook on life has a huge impact on your success.
Meaningful	Strive for something that means a lot to you. Could also stand for Memorable.
Stability	Does not let challenges knock you off track, stay **S**table. And do not forget to **S**mile.

Ask yourself these additional questions and write your answers below:

Am I on the right track?

Have I laid a solid foundation?

Is the path one-way?

Am I going around in circles?

Do I see my journey through life as a straight road? (Most often it is not)

How will I react when I reach a roadblock?

Is there room to expand and extend my track/goal?

When will I start this journey?

Do I have a timetable?

Do I have a map?

Who is with me? (team, partner, coach)

Do I have a destination in mind?

What is at this destination?

Why am I going there?

Am I in the driver's seat or relaxing up the back?

Am I determined to last the distance?

Will I stay on board even when the journey is an uphill struggle?

Is there anything hanging on and holding me back?

Am I willing to let it go?

We all need someone to help us get on the right track and keep us there when the going gets tough, so you might consider engaging a life coach.

You have probably set goals for yourself in the past, started with great enthusiasm and then discovered that willpower alone was not enough. I am going to share with you something more powerful than willpower that will encourage you to strive for your dreams.

Internal driver

David McClelland author of *The Achieving Society* highlights the significance of our 'internal driver' through his cognitive theory.

He discovered that for some people, the thought of accomplishing tasks and advancing in their role is enough to drive them forward in life. They also thrive on the idea of ticking off the next goal and being promoted.

For others, the feeling of power, having an impact and gaining status is all it takes to get them up and to run. And for the third group, their driver is all about association. These people love to interact with individuals, to share with communities and to promote teamwork.

Do you know what drives you? Is it achievement, authority, or affiliation?

Note that your internal driver can change based on the circumstances. For example, at work, you may be driven by praise and money, but at home, you are more driven by a sense of belonging. It is especially important to listen to what motivates you; otherwise, your life can become a journey of daily drudgery.

A friend of mine, who was a hospital doctor, loved helping his patients. He prided himself on his relationship with them. When offered a promotion, he took it, motivated by the idea of earning more money. However, sitting behind a desk doing paperwork all day, left him feeling hugely dissatisfied. He missed his patients and the feeling of helping and connecting with others. Make sure to get in touch with your internal driver when making life decisions.

Our internal driver may propel us forward at the start of our journey, but as human beings, we need practical tools to help us keep going. That is why every new development has a blueprint, a pattern, or a plan to follow.

I help all my clients create a schedule that they know they can keep up with, for as long as it takes to achieve their goal. For example, I allowed myself one month to write this book. I broke that allocated time into four weekly chunks and wrote down exactly what I needed to achieve during each week. I then divided those weeks into daily and hourly time slots. I listed relevant tasks to be undertaken during those periods. This made everything manageable and gave me the confidence I needed to know that I could achieve all I had set out to do.

One big lesson I have learned is that you will never find time to do everything you want. You must make time. On my calendar for this project, I first excluded the hours where I had non-negotiable commitments, that is, client appointments. Next, I wrote in the activities that are important to me, that is, my fitness class. Then I highlighted all the gaps and wrote a task in each one-hour slot. You will be surprised at how many hours you can claim for your project when you do this. I also made the decision to stop watching TV Monday – Thursday evenings, which gave me an extra 35 hours per month!

Chapter 9
The struggle is essential for growth

It is easy to *talk* about taking back control of your life. We have all heard friends or colleagues wax lyrical about their dreams.

It is also easy to *think* about taking back control of your life. Every day there are things that we think we would like to strive for in our life.

The challenging part is *doing* when taking back control of your life.

Doing is another way of saying that you will take consistent daily action towards your goal, even when you feel tired and overwhelmed.

We like to believe that getting what we want in life depends on luck or being in the right place at the right time, but this type of thinking is not realistic. Action is vital. Let us take a look at the necessary action that will help you achieve your dream.

I say necessary action because we can find ourselves busy but not productive. It is imperative to spend your time and energy on activities that are going to create great results.

When we did the visualisation exercise in Chapter 4, you created an imaginary picture of your future. After seeing yourself having achieved your goals, you floated back to the present.

What we did not do was to stop regularly. At various stages, look to see what you were doing at each point in time to achieve the desired result.

The final picture did not just magically appear. You made it happen. You created it with your imagination, and you will bring it to life with your motivation and determination.

Action

Motivation is a word that can be split into two: motive and action. Your motive is the reason behind what you want – it is why you want what you want. However, just wanting it is not enough. Without action, your motive will remain a dream. Your motive creates action, and together they create positive results.

Determination is another word that can be split into two: determined and action. To be determined is to be committed, to let nothing and no one get in your way.

We all love watching videos on YouTube of babies attempting to climb out of their cots, crawl up steep stairs, or walk alone for the first time. Why do these intrigue us? These babies amaze us because they show no fear, and they do not give up; they stumble, fall and slip, but they do not give up! They learn from each trial and use this learning to develop their next effort.

It is worth noting that the person recording the video is usually quiet (and may even be hiding). So, there is no one telling the baby to "be careful; take it easy, stop trying." As a result, they get to experience the joy and satisfaction that comes with overcoming obstacles in life.

This leads me to ask the questions, "when did you lose your childhood determination?" And "why did you lose your childish determination?" Write your personal answers here:

Maybe your parents reflected their own fear onto you. Maybe your teachers were keen to keep you in your place. Whatever the reasons, it is now time for you to reclaim that right, to take back control of your life and live the future you desire.

Our thoughts can be pessimistic and our language negative, however, the good news is that they can both be silenced by action. Our thinking can sabotage our routine by letting us off the hook or distracting us with other activities. We must silence those thoughts, and we do this by consciously allowing our physiology to be in control. We can override subconscious thoughts that cause indecision and procrastination.

As mentioned before, you cannot trust your feelings, and you will rarely feel like doing what must be done. So, when you have a project to complete or a job to finish, I recommend that you become a robot. Why? Because robots do not have feelings, they are programmed. They do not think; they do not ponder; they do not second-guess themselves; they just perform the task at hand.

"I'm trying my best," I hear you say, "but I'm just not getting anywhere." Well, that is because trying does not work. Imagine if I dropped a pencil and then said I would try and pick it up. It does not make sense. Either I bend down, curl my fingers around it and remove it from the ground; or I do not!

I am sure you have experienced a friend telling you that she will 'try' and make it to your party on Saturday night. As soon as she says those words, you know that she is not going to show up. The same applies to desired outcomes in any area of your life. Every success starts by deciding, and long-lasting success comes from consistent action. I challenge you to remove the word 'try' from your vocabulary and make your 'yes' a yes and your 'no' a no!

Rituals and routine

Repetitive behaviours, otherwise known as habits, have a huge impact on our life. We all have habits that we have formed over time, some more positive than others. We enjoy things when we are good at them, and we get good at them by repeated practice. The secret ingredient to taking back control of your life is routine.

Check this list of good habits, which of them do you employ in your daily life?

- Regular sleep.
- Healthy eating plan.
- Accepting of others.
- Uplifting relationships.
- Calm, positive thoughts.
- Time to relax and socialise.
- Financial savings structure.
- Community involvement/volunteering.

What bad habits do you currently have that you would like to stop?

- Fear.
- Irritated all the time.
- Judgmental of others.
- Ongoing financial worries.
- Start and never finish tasks.
- Recurring feelings of loneliness.
- Weight loss, weight regain, repeat.
- Attracting the wrong type of partner.
- Always being too busy or having no time.
- Recurring conflicts around the same topics.
- Constant struggles with relationships at home and, or work.
- Addiction: food, alcohol, shopping, sex, cigarettes, computer.

While all the patterns listed above vary in severity and nature, they all have one thing in common. That commonality is a tendency to recur in one's life, be it daily, monthly, or annually.

Client stories

What is interesting is that most of us know the bad habits that we have, but few of us question why we continue to own them. For example, my client Theresa was a yo-yo dieter, and no matter how hard she tried, she could not keep the excess weight off.

Delving deep into the core of the issue, we eventually uncovered the fact that she came from a large, low-income family, and when she was young food was scarce. From the age of four, she learned to hoard and hide food. Forty years later, she was still doing the same thing even though she had an abundance of everything she could ever need. When she realized that she was still living that old habit, she did not know whether to laugh or cry!

Emily, a successful businesswoman whom I coached, always complained and worried about a lack of money. I found this hard to believe because I knew she had a high paid job.

Through discussion, I discovered that she supported many charities and was very generous towards friends and family. We found that her underlying issue was approval. She wanted to be liked and thought of as a kind and generous person. She unwittingly used the money to impress people, and when she had no money, she believed that she had no value and no self-worth. Eventually, she was able to love herself and now has far more to give than just money.

Which bad habit do you need to replace with an empowering pattern? Choose one main thing to start working on in your life. Make a note of it here and the steps to change it today.

It is a known fact that the more pleasure you feel while learning a new habit, the more likely you will be to repeat it and thus the habit will stick. With the habit you noted above, listen to music you love while performing this new action or walk somewhere beautiful, or stroke your cheek. Be kind to yourself while striving for change.

We all want quick change, but that is not how the universe works. Instead, we are rewarded by long term commitment. Routine is the secret to taking back control of your life.

If we want a baby to sleep, we are advised to adopt a bedtime routine, so the baby becomes accustomed to going to bed at a certain time and knows what to expect next. When we are a student, we have the routine of attending lessons every day; this helps us to stay focused and build our learning. When at the gym, we are given an exercise routine to work all parts of the body, and we get stronger each time we complete the routine.

Life is a marathon, not a sprint; take it one step at a time and stay excited about the road ahead.

I would like to finish this chapter with an analogy about the journey of an emperor moth. I do not know who wrote this story, but I am thankful for the lesson it teaches, and I want to share it with you.

A man found a cocoon of an emperor moth. He took it home so that he could watch it come out of the cocoon.

One day a small opening appeared, he sat and watched the moth for several hours as it struggled to force its body through the little hole. After a while, it seemed to stop making any progress; it appeared that it had gotten as far as it could and could not go any further. It seemed to be stuck.

The man, in his kindness, decided to help the moth. With a pair of scissors, he snipped off the remaining bit of the cocoon. The moth then emerged with ease. It had a swollen body and small, shrivelled wings.

The man continued to watch the moth because he expected, at any moment, its wings would enlarge and expand to be able to support the bloated body. He was sure it would contract soon. Neither happened! In fact, the little moth spent the rest of its life crawling around with a swollen body and shrivelled wings. It was never able to fly.

What the man in his haste had not understood was that the restricting the cocoon and the struggle, required for the moth to get through the tiny opening was nature's way of forcing fluid from the moth's body into its wings. This was so it would be ready for flight once it achieved freedom from the cocoon.

Freedom and flight would only come after the struggle. Depriving the moth of this struggle, the man unwittingly deprived it of health and its natural body.

Sometimes struggles are essential in life. If we go through life without overcoming obstacles, we can get stuck in our comfort zone and slowly die having never truly lived.

We deprive ourselves of a sense of achievement, accomplishment, and the opportunity to grow. If we do not have setbacks and failures, we have nothing to compare the good times in our life.

We may inadvertently cripple others and ourselves emotionally, leaving us fearing life and its challenges. It is an especially important step in the early development of a child to experience and learn from challenges because then they can celebrate when they achieve their own breakthroughs. It is up to us to help ourselves, and thus by example, help those around us to develop. Let us all strive to be physically, emotionally, and mentally as strong as we can be.

Chapter 10
Life is all about relationships

If you look back throughout your life, you will probably agree that the most difficult times were due to dysfunctional relationships.

From today onwards, please accept that *you are in charge of your relationships*. We can blame other people, but at some point, we must take a close look at our own thoughts, words, and actions in any relationship. We must recognise the negative influence we may have had, even if unintentional. Relationships are two-way, and no one person is ever responsible for total failure.

In life, no matter what we want, we always need other people to help us practically or emotionally. I do not mean 'using' other people, I am talking about the inter-connectedness of human beings.

Some may disagree with this and say, "I do not need anyone; I do things by myself because only I can do it to the standard that I like." Maybe you control how you run your life, including your career, family, health, and wealth, but you do not do everything by yourself.

As the famous poet John Donne quoted, "No man is an island."

From our birth, we are connected to family and community. We may choose to break verbal and physical communication with people that disagree with us. However, ultimately, we are still part of the same bloodline. Without relationships, we shrivel up and die emotionally.

Couples who are having a problematic relationship come to me complaining that their partner does not give enough; they are both saying the same thing! Situations like these require both parties to change their desires from one of getting to one of giving.

I dream of the day I hear two people say that their partner just keeps on giving. I do not mean material gifts; I mean giving of themselves, their time, their love, and their interest in the other. These are the things we all yearn for, yet these are also the things we forget to give.

We think we do not have enough time or energy or money to give to those around us. Often clients will say to me, "Why should I bother? It will not be reciprocated or appreciated."

Giving to receive never works because firstly, people cannot read your mind and do not know that you are expecting something in return. Secondly, cloaked generosity prevents the natural flow of reciprocity. I tell you now, give as much as you can because YOU will feel better!

Giving, sharing, and loving unconditionally positively impacts our own life as adrenaline. If you do not believe me, try it.

Write down three things that you could do for someone today to show them that you care and then write how this act of kindness made YOU feel.

Kind Acts

I felt

Linear relationships

Since the beginning of time, human beings have always judged one another. In fact, scientific reports prove that we make up our mind about someone within the first seven seconds of meeting them.

Part of this judgment is the hierarchy system that we create in our head. We tend to place others either above or below ourselves. We see them as either richer or poorer than ourselves, smarter or dumber than ourselves, prettier or uglier than ourselves, funnier or more serious than ourselves. We subconsciously rank everyone we meet based on our perception of the world and our own standards.

I would like to share with you the idea of linear relationships. By this, I mean that everyone has an equal opportunity to strive for whatever they want. Each person has self-confidence and faith in their own ability, plus they can recognise talent in others.

People in control of their own life do not feel the need to compare. They do not see every component of life as a competition, and they believe in everyone striving for their individual, personal best.

Those who see all adults as equals and welcome those who are different have much happier, longer-lasting relationships.

My parents taught me to put others first, to share, to give my time and money to charity, to pray for those less fortunate. I loved these values. However, I got a shock when I started working in the real world. I discovered that not everyone was friendly, accepting or kind. Worse still, kindness was synonymous with weakness!

What I learned during my journey of personal development (which is ongoing) was that in trying to please everyone else,

I had lost sight of myself. In fact, I did not think I was entitled to want and desire – because that is what selfish people did.

What I now know is that it does not have to be selfless, selfish, giving, taking, or all or nothing. Life is all about balance, a bit for you and a bit for me. I am an adult with ambitions and am fulfilling them. I also now have more to offer those around me because I feel satisfied with life.

The biggest lesson I learned was to stop asking for permission. I see so many women give their power to others through their desire for approval. If consent is not granted, then you might go ahead and do your own thing anyway. Then the other person feels disgruntled and angry. So, either way, you do not win.

Your life is your life. We are each on this planet to discover our God-given talents, to celebrate our successes, to deal with our sorrows and to be guardians of everything around us. I am not promoting thoughtlessness. I am highlighting the need for everyone to take responsibility for her own life and future.

Let me encourage you to develop awareness. Accept that no two people see or experience the world the same; acknowledge that our world is continually changing and agree that different does not mean wrong.

Fear of the unknown or the unusual is what creates pain in the world. Lack of understanding and willingness to accept change is what causes arguments in a marriage. The need to be right is what causes disputes in the workplace.

The most important relationship is the one you have with yourself. We change the world by first changing ourselves, changing our own inner world, learning, developing, and growing by acquiring new skills and accepting new ideas. Then change our outer world, how we see the world and how our thoughts, words and actions can make for a better world.

We are human beings, not human doings. So, let us just be. Be yourself and allow others to be who they were created to be. Be a good role model for your children and allow them to be courageous and adventurous in their life.

Digital relationships

What would your family say about your relationship with social media and online friendships? I know it is not practical these days to opt-out of technology entirely. The web and digital devices are now thoroughly integrated into our modern world. And to be honest, I love using Facebook as a means for keeping in touch with my family overseas. I was recently 'found' on Facebook by old school friends that I had not seen for 30 years. Words cannot describe the excitement I felt at being reconnected with them.

However, the digital world can be all-consuming for our children and us. It can damage family relationships if we do not take control of it. Here are a few things I recommend to clients, so social media does not rule their life or take over precious family time.

- Check your email only twice a day maximum, unless your work is based entirely on the email, of course!
- Do not click any social media sites until you have completed other important tasks for the day.
- Get rid of notifications and alerts.
- Declutter your desktop; it helps relieve being overwhelmed.
- Uninstall software/apps you do not use anymore.
- Use bookmarks to host similar topics.
- Unsubscribe from sites you do not engage with anymore.
- Stop using the Internet after 10 pm each day (it disturbs sleep patterns if used before bedtime).

As parents, we have a significant influence on our children. Often, we feel this is not true because it appears that they never listen or do what they are told. Do not be fooled; they are watching, and often subconsciously, copying your behaviour. There is no point shouting at them to turn off their digital gadgets if you are staring at your phone. It is more powerful to teach by example.

Because there is so much activity online, children can often feel that being online *is* their life. It is our job as parents to remind them that the internet is a 'tool' to enhance our lives with easy access to music, recipes, and teachings, but it is not our life. It is a network that links people together. It facilitates connection on a surface level. It can never give us the things we enjoy in real life: a warm hug, a delicious hot chocolate, or the smell of freshly cut grass.

Family life is fun and rewarding when built on clear, caring communication. As your children mature, it is important to make time to connect with them on a personal level, every day. Organise a walk, have an ice-cream or play family football at the park. If you must stay indoors, start a game of cards, and invite them to join you rather than playing digital games individually. Every reward in life requires effort, and if you do not put effort into your family habits now, you will not reap the rewards later.

With so many social networks and messaging apps, that is Facebook; WhatsApp; Snapchat; Instagram and Twitter, it can often feel like we have been taken over by them. You will have witnessed the change from the days of the everyday old cassette player. Still, to your children, technology is normal. They cannot understand why we think it is disruptive as they have never known anything else.

A great idea is to hold a weekly family meeting. We started doing this when our girls were at primary school. Every Sunday afternoon, we would put aside an hour or so to discuss the forthcoming week. We would also mark everyone's activities on a communal calendar. In doing this, we would ask what we each needed help with and offered at least one contribution each to make family life more positive. The kids enjoyed taking turns writing the 'minutes of the meeting', and afterwards, we would all play a board game together. At your family meeting, why not get each person to think consciously about all the social platforms they use; and to agree to drop the ones that do not add value.

Chapter 11
It is not what you say, it is the way that you say it!

'*Think before you speak,*' is a well-known phrase. The influence of language is so powerful that we should all heed this cautionary saying.

Do you know that the words you use can have an incredible impact on how others perceive you, and how you feel about yourself? Your mind chatters all the time, so it is important to be aware of what you are saying to yourself regularly.

Often the way we speak to ourselves is worse than anything we would ever say to someone else. Without realising it, we sabotage our ability to take back control of our lives because this negative language sends disempowering messages to the brain and body.

Clear communication is essential in all walks of life, don't you agree? Almost anything we strive for involves the co-operation of others. So, it is imperative to have awareness around how you ask for support.

This alone can make a difference between others wanting to help you and not. If your communication style is aggressive, or self-centred, you are less likely to get the support you seek, than if your style is endearing.

When we were younger many of us were told to, "Be quiet. Wait until you are spoken to. No one asked for your opinion!" Or we were shamed for asking a silly question and ridiculed for not knowing the answer. This has caused many adults to retreat verbally, to keep their opinions to themselves and become passive in their communication style. This has gone on to harm their relationships at home and work.

Both aggressive and passive communication hinder your true message. To be heard and understood, you need to learn, and it is a skill that can be learned, to be assertive. Assertiveness just means learning to communicate your needs, wants, feelings, opinions and beliefs honestly and directly, without intentionally hurting anyone's feelings.

There are many benefits to being assertive:

- More in Control
- Being more tactful
- Improves credibility
- Increases self-confidence
- Feel good about self and others
- Others feel more positive about you

It is important to tell those who love you what you want, how you plan to go about getting it, and how they can support you. This is a powerful step towards achieving your ambitions. People cannot read your mind, and they do not know how to help you if you do not tell them.

Most women I work with are generous of spirit and are quick to offer a helping hand whenever needed. Still, they are terrible at asking for help in return. Asking for help is not a weakness; it is a strength. Being aware of your own limitations, be it time or skill, is a positive attribute. Do not deny others the joy of helping you, and the feeling of being needed.

If you are clear, honest, and kind in all your communications, you will thrive in relationships and find it easier to get what you want from life.

I like this quote from Alice in Wonderland, *'say what you mean and mean what you say'* and I say to do this without being mean.

How would you rate your current communication skills?

How would others rate your communication skills?

I like to talk, whether in person, via skype, delivering presentations or training workshops. I feel frustrated when people do not get what I am trying to say, and I hate to admit it, but it's not their fault - it's mine!

I know this because, for many years, I have been interested in the work of Professor Albert Mehrabian. His research provides the basis for the much-quoted statistic below. These findings highlight the effectiveness, (or lack of) when using the spoken word to communicate feelings and attitudes:

- 7% of meaning is the words that are spoken;
- 38% of meaning is the way that words are said and or attitude;
- 55% of meaning is in facial expression.

So, even though people may hear the words you are saying. They are more influenced by what they see you saying. Incredibly, 93% of what you say is not really being heard!

We often communicate without using words at all; here are a few examples:

- The way we look at someone (judgmental).
- The way we look away from someone (ignoring them).
- Hand gestures (thumbs up, or rude finger).
- Our face changes in colour (embarrassed or angry).
- We cannot look someone in the eye (shy or hiding the truth).

- Honk the horn on the steering wheel when irritated in heavy.
- Traffic.
- Scratch our heads when puzzled.

And sometimes we communicate using our tone of voice:

- High pitched (excited or anxious)
- Growling (annoyed or tired)
- Huffing (disappointed or displeased)
- Low and slow (calming a situation)

I know these examples are generalisations and we do have to be careful with our interpretation of others' behaviour so that we do not wrongly misjudge them. For example, someone sitting at a company meeting with their arms folded tightly may just be cold not necessarily disengaged or distant.

It is important to take the content and the context of someone's message into account when assessing their body language and to look for congruence.

If someone is genuine and honest, you will feel, hear, and see a synergy between their words, intentions and actions. And remember people will also be looking for this from you.

Body language

Alan Pease has studied human body communication for decades. He shares his discoveries in his best-selling book: *The Definitive Book of Body Language.* I recommend this book to help you become aware of the signals you instinctively give out. When you understand what this is, you can communicate effectively with loved ones, work colleagues and anyone else. Throughout his book Pease gives many examples of 'signals', some are physical, others are perceived, and many are facial. The one I love the most is the smile:

"The smile is the universal expression of happiness. As children, we were often encouraged to put on a 'happy face'. It was good advice because smiling tends to encourage a positive response in others. Most people cannot tell the difference between a genuine smile – which produces characteristic wrinkles around the eyes – and a false smile, which only involves the mouth muscles.

And smiles – fake or genuine – are contagious. Research has proven that it is nearly impossible not to smile at someone who smiles at you – and this creates positive feelings in both of you. Smiling and laughing have been scientifically shown to have beneficial social and health effects. Smiling people are more popular, receive more positive feedback from others and suffer fewer ulcers! Laughter stimulates the body's natural endorphins, which relaxes the body and relieves pain while strengthening the immune system."

Our body language sends out a message to the world - confident or shy, success or failure, happy or sad. People can read our mood by the way we walk into a room. Before we say a word, they can tell if we are excited or bored, just by our physiology.

Look around you now. Do you notice those who people look tired, dishevelled, and slumped over? Do you compare their stance to those who are walking tall and have a smile on their face? What is your physiology telling the world about you today?

The positive response comes when we foster a natural rapport with someone. If you are negotiating, with your partner or boss, and their body language is distant and cold, fighting or copying that behaviour will lead to further negativity and misunderstanding.

If you want to get them back on your side, you must break their posture, which will interrupt their negative thoughts and give you a chance to renegotiate. So how do you do this?

Distract them by pointing out something irrelevant to the conversation, that is, the room is too hot, and you must open the window. Or give them something, maybe a pen and paper and ask them to write down their complaints. Offer them a cup of tea, not only is this a positive gesture, but it will also break their stance when they reach out to take the cup.

If sitting, you could lean forward, with your palms open and invite them to ask you a question. By doing this, you are taking control of the situation in a positive way. If you have your palms up, you are indicating you are open to resolving the situation. Your invitation allows for reciprocation.

One thing that is difficult to hide when genuine is facial expression. We automatically blush when we are embarrassed. Our eyelids blink when we are confused or trying to hide something. The pupils of our eyes dilate when telling lies and our hands tend to go sweaty when nervous.

On the other hand, when you are in alignment with a good friend or partner, you both tend to perform some actions at the same time without even realising it. Often, my husband and I will unintentionally pick up our wine glass to drink at the same time. Or I will notice that my friend and I are sitting crossed legged with our heads tilted in the same direction.

With people, if you struggle to create rapport you do not know but would really like to, then one suggestion is to 'mirror' their behaviour. This must be done in a relaxed, natural manner. Otherwise, you may come across as being a bit creepy!

I am not suggesting that you act like someone you are not. Authenticity is far more important. But maybe you have lost sight of your true self and are unintentionally sending out misleading signals to those around you. Maybe you have forgotten about the spring in your step, or how you used to look people in the eye.

Take a moment to reflect on your behaviour, your outlook, and your language, then write a list of improvements to implement into your action plan.

The language that people use sometimes provide insight into how they think. Most of us fall into one of four categories: audio, visual, kinaesthetic or audio-digital (self-talk). When listening to another, pay attention to the senses they describe when talking, for example:

- I see what you mean
- I hear what you say
- I feel bad about that
- I am very touched by your thoughtfulness
- What you are telling me is distasteful
- Interesting, isn't it?

Chapter 12
Let go and grow

You may remember that in Chapter 3, I mentioned that at the top of Maslow's hierarchy of needs, humans seek self-realisation. This means being at one with ourselves and the world around us. We think of this as being in control, but it is more about letting go. I would like to share a short story that illustrates the importance of letting go.

In a small village in Thailand, a monkey ran riot; stealing, destroying and annoying the people.

One day, the village chief announced that he had a plan to trap the monkey. He cut a small hole at the top of a coconut, an opening big enough for the monkey to put its hand inside. He then emptied the coconut milk and placed some peanuts inside the coconut shell and left it where the monkey could find it.

The monkey was delighted when he smelled the peanuts. He stuck his hand inside the coconut shell and attempted to steal the peanuts. But with a clenched fist, he could not get his hand back out. Unable to fight or run fast with the heavy coconut attached to his arm, the monkey was caught.

All that silly monkey had to do was let go of the peanuts. If he had opened his fist and dropped the peanuts, he would have been able to pull his hand back out, but he was not willing to let go of the peanuts and so remained trapped.

There is an excellent lesson for us to learn through this story. Take a moment to answer the following questions.

What are you holding on to that is keeping you trapped?

What would it take for you to let go?

We can often be like that monkey; running around crazy and unintentionally creating havoc. In fact, it almost seems popular these days to tell everyone how busy we are. But this is not something to be proud of in life. It is important to take time out and focus on your life.

I recently went on a yoga retreat. It was a wonderful time for self-reflection and nurturing. I was looking after myself, so I could continue to look after others and all areas of my life. I ate healthy food, drank lots of freshwater, slept well, walked among nature, and took time to be grateful for each moment.

When did you last treat yourself to a time of relaxation?

When did you last let go and allow yourself space to grow?

During this retreat, one of the teachers shared a meditation written by Safire Rose, and I want to share it with you because it sums up everything I want to say in this chapter.

She let go.

Without a thought or a word, she let go.

She let go of the fear.

She let go of the judgments.

She let go of the confluence of opinions swarming around her head.

She let go of the committee of indecision within her.

She let go of all the 'right' reasons.

Wholly and completely, without hesitation or worry, she just let go.

She did not ask anyone for advice.

She did not read a book on how to let go.

She did not search all the scriptures; she just let go.

She let go of all the memories that held her back.

She let go of all the anxiety that kept her from moving forward.

She let go of all the calculations about how to do it right.

She did not promise to let go.

She did not journal about it.

She did not write the projected date in her diary.

She made no public announcement and put no ad in the newspaper.

She did not analyse whether she should let go.

She did not call her friends to discuss the matter.

She did not utter a word; she just let go.

No one was around when it happened.

There was no applause or congratulations.

No one thanked her or praised her.

No one noticed a thing.

Like a leaf falling from a tree, she just let go.

There was no effort.

There was no struggle.

It was not good, and it was not bad.

It was what it was, and it is just that.

In the space of letting go, she let it all be.

A small smile came over her face.

A light breeze blew through her.

And the sun and the moon shone.

Chapter 13
Track your progress

Do you write a regular journal? Is it a 'dear diary' list of daily trials or a notebook full of your achievements and dreams?

Recent research shows that it is no longer recommended as healthy to write about what is bad and sad in your life. This is because the more you focus on any situation, the deeper it becomes etched in your memory. To help you move on, you are advised to write only one short sentence about the 'negative issue' to get it off your chest. This will help you have a cheerier outlook. Immediately tear it up, throw it away and list lots of ways to overcome it.

An exercise I encourage my clients to undertake is known as 3x3x3. This involves taking three minutes, three times a day, to write down three things that make you smile. This not only gives the mind a moment to pause and reflect but also fills it with positive images, which create positive emotions and leads to a more positive outlook.

You know that at the start of each new year, we are encouraged to throw away old calendars and start fresh with a blank canvass. We make resolutions to change and improve. We make verbal commitments to others and ourselves.

By mid-February, when we do not measure up, we label ourselves as a failure and give up completely, stating that it was all too difficult.

Life is difficult. Sticking to new resolutions is difficult. Changing bad habits is difficult. Being positive and productive every day is difficult. But it is not impossible. We need to accept this and give ourselves a reality check. We can then begin to see that one small step towards a fulfilling purpose each day is better than huge goals that overwhelm and defeat us.

As you start this new phase of your life, be proud of the fact that you want to set some higher standards for yourself. Remain realistic with your expectations of yourself and others. When our expectations are based on wishful thinking, we often end up disappointed and frustrated. And remember that instant gratification, which may bring temporary gain, is often not sustainable.

Most successful people will tell you they got where they are by embracing hard work, integrity, honesty, and trust in their dealings and relationships.

The key to taking back control of your life is to recognise the obstacles that you face in achieving your goal. You also need to set out to overcome them, take daily action and focus on your wins, no matter how small.

If you invest in your own personal development, you will see great progress. This includes growing a positive support team around you, maximising your strengths, and recognising the talents of others.

You will recognise your growth when you find yourself sharing what you have learned with others. A great way to track your progress is by seeking feedback. Others are always willing to give us their opinions. If you are open to listening and receiving this feedback without taking it personally, you can use it to track your progress.

Your emotional state is also a great way to measure your progress. If you look forward to each new day, spurred on by your dream, then you can be sure you are on the right track.

Life is unpredictable. New challenges and opportunities arise every day. We need to have awareness and to be discerning, so always ask yourself, "Is this a distraction or something that will help me achieve my goal?" Learning to make good choices comes from experience and experience brings wisdom. We can study principles and read about the experiences of others. Still, the place where you will truly develop discernment and wisdom is on your own journey.

Balance is another way to track your progress. If your personal needs are being met and your work goals are on track, but your family life is a mess, then maybe you are not as successful as you think.

I am sure we all know people who have material riches and no time for one another. They also have no time for others who give totally to the family but lack self-esteem.

Before the industrialisation of society, most works were done in or near the home, children learned from their parents and work was a bonding experience.

In the modern world, paid work is outside the home and work inside the home being devalued. With a little imagination, we can build bridges between our work (whether in the home or not) and home life.

Talk to family members about your dreams and goals. Help them to understand the challenges you face, include them when celebrating your achievements. When we see both work and home as avenues for contribution and satisfaction, we move beyond complaints and compromise to complementary and balanced.

One of the greatest gifts we have is time, yet many see it as the enemy. We rush against time; we have no time to share, we cannot make time, or buy time. We let time dominate us and use it as an excuse to express frustration and anxiety. It is said that the way we use our time reflects what is most important to us in life. Do you track how you use your time?

Everyone has the same 24 hours each day, so how come some are relaxed and successful while others are not? They make time work for them. They divide their time, they plan their time, and they do not waste their time. They know that times flies, and they are the pilot.

Another way to track your progress is through money. Money is a communicator of value. Companies and households are run by it and can be ruined by a lack of it. We all spend a considerable amount of energy earning money, spending money, and managing money. Our attitude towards money has a huge impact on our success in life.

Is money an emotional issue for you?

What do you spend your money on?

What does this say about you?

Do you have a financial plan?

How much money do you really need to live a balanced, happy life?

People who deal effectively with money see its long-term value. They look to invest rather than consume. Most wealthy entrepreneurs do not keep working to earn more money; they do it for fun. They enjoy what they do, and they enjoy the freedom money offers.

We can have a lot of fun with money. I do not mean that you should buy symbols of wealth. Instead, volunteer in a third world country, invest in a new venture that improves the world for all, contribute to an invention, or sponsor a young, bright mind.

In my work as a life coach. I have seen spending decisions create division and be a source of great pain in relationships. With your partner, take time to create a shared financial strategy for all areas of your life. Look for ways to grow your money and teach your children to do the same.

When tracking your progress, do not forget to include measures for both your body and mind. They are so intrinsically connected that when one is out of balance, it adversely affects the other.

The essentials are plenty of clean drinking water, whole foods, regular exercise, daily affirmations, prayer or meditation, reading, restful sleep, volunteering and do not forget smiling.

Lastly, you will know when your life is in control because of how you feel on the inside. When you are on the right track, making progress and enjoying life, you will feel joyful, energetic, and empowered. This is the litmus test of life. This is when you know you have let go.

Chapter 14
A helping hand

Taking back control of your life is difficult and doing it on your own is tough.

Why do you think Olympians, executives, supermodels, and entrepreneurs all have a life coach? Because they know the value of having guidance, techniques that work and continued support. They also know that a coach is:

- Someone who puts you first.
- Someone who listens to your dreams.
- Someone who helps you achieve those dreams.
- Someone determined to see you succeed.
- Someone who cheers you on from the sidelines.
- Someone who knows how to dig deeper to get the best out of you.
- Someone who sees potential in you that you may not see in yourself.

I believe everyone deserves a life coach. We all have an athlete, showman, author, or entrepreneur inside us. We just need a coach to help us uncover the layers of learned behaviour that prevent us from achieving our true potential.

So where to from here? If you have ever thought of having a life coach, but are not sure if it is right for you, there is only one way to find out. Book a time for us to have a chat and see if we are a good fit. If not, at least I can point you in the right direction.

What else? If you have found this book helpful, then please share it with others, so they too may benefit and can take back control of their life.

Keep in touch and up to date with all that is happening by following me on social media.

This is the link to my Website calendar

https://annemckeown.com/contact/

About the Author

Anne McKeown, from Scotland, lives in Sydney with her husband and two daughters. Anne is a highly regarded Master NLP coach who has dedicated her life to empowering women in business and life. Throughout her expansive career, she has worked in corporate, education and the charity sector.

Anne has had blogs and magazine articles published around her expertise as a Women's Empowerment Coach. She has also contributed guest chapters to books on the topics of Life Success and Having It All. To read these articles visit her website: https://www.annemckeown.com

Anne is the founder of 2Mpower.co. The name of her company encompasses her mission to empower women to step up, speak out, achieve their goals and live the life they were born to live. The 2Ms in 2Mpower are her daughters Maris and Megan, for whom she strives to be a good role model.

Anne offers coaching sessions for individuals and groups. She works with women seeking fulfilment, as well as female entrepreneurs and corporate leaders who want to turbo-charge their results.

Anne is often booked as a guest speaker.

If you or someone you know would like to find out more, she can be contacted at anne@2mpower.co and replies to every email.

www.ingramcontent.com/pod-product-compliance
Lightning Source LLC
Chambersburg PA
CBHW070729020526
44107CB00077B/2283